COUNTRY PROFILES

TANZANIA

BY GOLRIZ GOLKAR

D1606917

BLASTOFF! DISCOVERY

BELLWETHER MEDIA • MINNEAPOLIS, MN

Blastoff! Discovery launches a new mission: reading to learn. Filled with facts and features, each book offers you an exciting new world to explore!

BLASTOFF! UNIVERSE

BLASTOFF! Beginners — GRADE K

BLASTOFF! READERS — GRADES 1-3

DISCOVERY — GRADE 4

This edition first published in 2023 by Bellwether Media, Inc.

No part of this publication may be reproduced in whole or in part without written permission of the publisher.
For information regarding permission, write to Bellwether Media, Inc., Attention: Permissions Department,
6012 Blue Circle Drive, Minnetonka, MN 55343.

Library of Congress Cataloging-in-Publication Data

Names: Golkar, Golriz, author.
Title: Tanzania / by Golriz Golkar.
Other titles: Blastoff! discovery. Country profiles.
Description: Minneapolis : Bellwether Media, Inc., 2023. | Series: Blastoff! Discovery: Country profiles | Includes bibliographical references and index. | Audience: Ages 7-13 | Audience: Grades 4-6 | Summary: "Engaging images accompany information about Tanzania. The combination of high-interest subject matter and narrative text is intended for students in grades 3 through 8"–Provided by publisher.
Identifiers: LCCN 2022050040 (print) | LCCN 2022050041 (ebook) | ISBN 9798886871500 (library binding) | ISBN 9798886872767 (ebook)
Subjects: LCSH: Tanzania–Juvenile literature. | Tanzania–Social life and customs–Juvenile literature.
Classification: LCC DT438 .G56 2023 (print) | LCC DT438 (ebook) | DDC 967.8–dc23/eng/20221017
LC record available at https://lccn.loc.gov/2022050040
LC ebook record available at https://lccn.loc.gov/2022050041

Editor: Rachael Barnes   Designer: Brittany McIntosh

Printed in the United States of America, North Mankato, MN.

TABLE OF CONTENTS

A family visits the National Museum in Dar es Salaam. They see exhibits important to Tanzanian **culture** and human history. The family then heads to the bustling Kariakoo Market. Colorful stalls are packed tightly along the city streets. They sell everything from spices and food to clothing and home goods. The family buys **souvenirs**.

OTHER TOP SITES

KILIMANJARO NATIONAL PARK

LAKE MANYARA NATIONAL PARK

THE OLD FORT

SELOUS GAME RESERVE

For a street food lunch, they visit Coco Beach. Fried cassava with cabbage salad and *mshikaki*, or grilled meat skewers, make a tasty meal. They drink fresh-squeezed sugarcane juice as they stroll along the sandy beach. Local musicians play *muziki wa dansi*. This is Tanzania!

UGANDA

KENYA

LAKE VICTORIA

RWANDA

BURUNDI

MWANZA

ARUSHA

LAKE TANGANYIKA

DODOMA

TANZANIA

DEMOCRATIC REPUBLIC OF THE CONGO

ZAMBIA

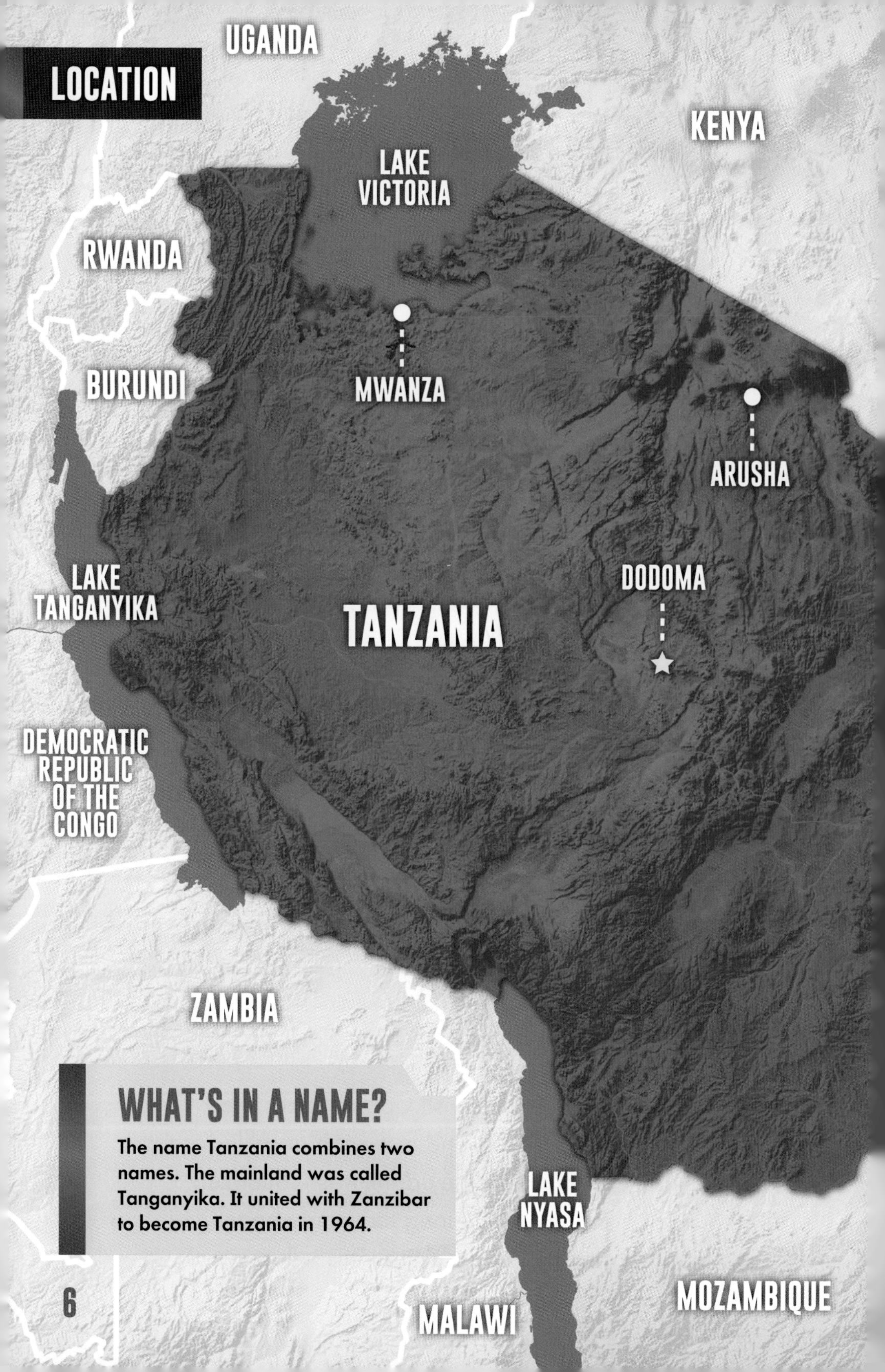

WHAT'S IN A NAME?

The name Tanzania combines two names. The mainland was called Tanganyika. It united with Zanzibar to become Tanzania in 1964.

LAKE NYASA

MOZAMBIQUE

MALAWI

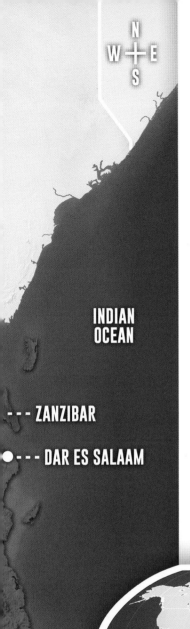

N
W + E
S

INDIAN
OCEAN

- - - ZANZIBAR

● - - - DAR ES SALAAM

Tanzania is located in eastern Africa. It covers 365,755 square miles (947,300 square kilometers). The capital, Dodoma, lies in the central region.

Lake Tanganyika fills the border between **mainland** Tanzania and the Democratic Republic of the Congo. Burundi and Rwanda lie to the northwest. Uganda and Kenya are northern neighbors. Lake Victoria lies where the three nations meet. The Indian Ocean stretches along the east. Many islands, including the Zanzibar **Archipelago**, lie near the coast. Mozambique, Lake Nyasa, Malawi, and Zambia surround the southern and southwestern border.

LANDSCAPE AND CLIMATE

Tanzania's famous Kilimanjaro stands tall in the northeast. But much of the landscape is split by two deep valleys. Lake Tanganyika fills part of the Western Rift Valley. The Great Rift Valley cuts through the center of the country. In between, the Serengeti **Plain** stretches across the north. It lies on a large central **plateau**. Grasslands make up the southern half of the country, while low plains meet the eastern coastline.

KILIMANJARO

LAKE TANGANYIKA

N W E S

= WESTERN RIFT VALLEY
= GREAT RIFT VALLEY

TALLEST MOUNTAIN

Kilimanjaro is sometimes called the roof of Africa. It is the tallest freestanding mountain in the world! A freestanding mountain is not part of a mountain range.

GREAT RIFT
VALLEY

DODOMA

Average
seasonal highs
and lows

JANUARY
HIGH: 85 °F (29 °C)
LOW: 67 °F (20 °C)

APRIL
HIGH: 83 °F (28 °C)
LOW: 66 °F (19 °C)

JULY
HIGH: 78 °F (26 °C)
LOW: 58 °F (14 °C)

OCTOBER
HIGH: 85 °F (29 °C)
LOW: 64 °F (18 °C)

°F = degrees Fahrenheit
°C = degrees Celsius

Tanzania has a **tropical** climate. The coast is hot and
humid while the central plateau is more dry. Mountaintops
have cooler temperatures. Tanzania has rainy and dry seasons.
Rain falls the heaviest between December and May.

WILDLIFE

Tanzania is home to some big and colorful animals. Many are protected by the country's parks. Zebras, dik-diks, and kudus eat grasses and shrubs. African lions and cheetahs stalk them nearby, waiting for their next meal. Masai giraffes, the national animal, munch on tree leaves. African savanna elephants flap their ears to keep cool on the Serengeti Plain.

Hippopotamuses and crocodiles float in rivers and lakes. They share Lake Victoria with catfish and tilapia. Pemba green-pigeons and black-bellied starlings fly around Pemba Island. Red colobus monkeys swing in the forests of Zanzibar. Blue-spotted rays and whale sharks circle the island waters.

DIK-DIK

BLACK-BELLIED STARLING

AFRICAN LION

HOME SWEET HOME

Tanzania is home to about half of all African lions. Lions and many other animals are losing their homes due to farming, hunting, and other human activities. Wildlife organizations are working hard to protect them.

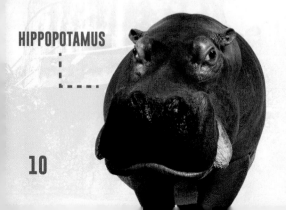

HIPPOPOTAMUS

MASAI
GIRAFFE

MASAI GIRAFFE

Life Span: 10 to 15 years
Red List Status: endangered

Masai giraffe range = ▮

LEAST CONCERN	NEAR THREATENED	VULNERABLE	ENDANGERED	CRITICALLY ENDANGERED	EXTINCT IN THE WILD	EXTINCT

Nearly 64 million people live in Tanzania. Small groups of people are from Asia and Europe. But almost every mainland Tanzanian has African **ancestors**. Most belong to one of the more than 100 Bantu **ethnic** groups in the country. Many **Arabs** live in Zanzibar. Some people in Zanzibar have African or both Arab and African ancestors.

Tanzanians speak Kiswahili, the official language of Tanzania. They also speak the language of their ethnic group. English is another official language used in schools and business. More than half of all Tanzanians are Christian. Most people who live in Zanzibar are Muslim.

FAMOUS FACE

Name: Saida Karoli
Birthday: April 4, 1976
Hometown: Bukoba, Tanzania
Famous for: A popular Tanzanian singer who performs traditional music throughout Africa

SPEAK KISWAHILI

ENGLISH	KISWAHILI	HOW TO SAY IT
hello	jambo	JOM-boh
goodbye	kwaheri	kwa-HEIR-ee
please	tafadhali	tah-fahd-HAH-lee
thank you	asante	ah-SAHN-tay
yes	ndiyo	in-DEE-yoh
no	hapana	hah-PAH-nah

ZANZIBAR

GROWING CITY

Dar es Salaam is the former capital of Tanzania. More than 7 million people lived there in 2022! It is the most populated Tanzanian city and one of the fastest-growing cities in the world.

DALA DALA

Many Tanzanians live in **rural** areas. They live in mud and brick huts with grass roofs. Electricity and clean, running water are uncommon. People travel on foot and by bicycle. **Urban** Tanzanians live in small concrete homes. People often share rooms. Buses, motorcycle taxis, and large vans called *dala dalas* help people get around cities. They drive on the left side of the road.

Tanzanians value family. They often live with or near extended family, especially in rural areas. Children leave home when they get married, graduate, or get a job. Adult children take care of aging parents.

Tanzanians are friendly. They shake hands when greeting others. Friends and family visit often. They are always offered food and drink.

TAARAB
PERFORMANCE

Music and dance are important to Tanzanian culture. They bring the community together for ceremonies and entertainment. *Ngoma* is lively drum music performed as people sing, dance, and tell stories. *Taarab* features string music played as performers sing poetry. The audience may sing, dance, and cheer along. *Bongo flava* is a newer popular music. It combines hip-hop and reggae styles with **traditional** Tanzanian music.

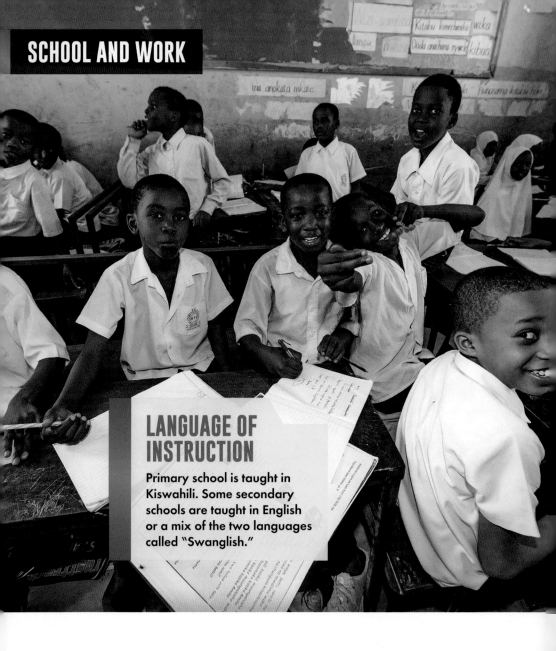

LANGUAGE OF INSTRUCTION

Primary school is taught in Kiswahili. Some secondary schools are taught in English or a mix of the two languages called "Swanglish."

Tanzanian children must attend primary school from ages 7 to 14. Public education is free. Starting at grade four, students must pass an exam to start the next grade. They attend secondary school for four years. Some students attend two more years of secondary school if they plan to go to university.

Many Tanzanians work on farms growing corn, rice, bananas, or nuts. Others work on large **plantations**. Common crops are coffee, cotton, or spices. The Maasai people are known for raising cattle. Some Tanzanians work in gold and gemstone mines. Others have jobs in offices, shops, or **tourism**.

TOURISM

MAASAI HERDER WITH THEIR CATTLE

SOCCER

Soccer is a favorite sport in Tanzania. Both children and adults enjoy playing. National soccer teams in Dar es Salaam and Dodoma often play friendly games. Some professional players are on international teams. Tennis, volleyball, and basketball are also popular sports. Girls especially enjoy netball, which is similar to basketball without dribbling.

NETBALL

Tanzanians enjoy traditional board games such as *bao*. Players move pebbles around a board and collect them to win. Urban dwellers may visit national parks on vacation. People in rural areas enjoy plays held during celebrations such as weddings or festivals.

BAO

FIRE ON THE MOUNTAIN

What You Need:
- two groups of people;
  an odd number of players is needed

What You Do:
1. Choose a leader. Make two even groups, an inner circle group and an outer circle group.
2. The inner circle group forms a circle around the leader. The outer circle group makes a larger circle around the inner circle group.
3. The leader calls out, "Fire on the mountain! Run, run, run!" The outer circle group must run around the inner circle group until the leader calls out, "Fire out!"
4. The leader and each player in the outer circle group must run to the inner circle group and partner with a player.
5. The player who is not fast enough to find a partner is the leader in the next round. The game begins again.
6. After three rounds, the inner and outer circles can switch roles.

MAKING
UGALI

Tanzanian **cuisine** is flavorful. It is often eaten with the hands. Rice, grains, and bananas are **staples**. *Ugali*, the national dish, is made from cooked cornmeal or other flour. Meats and fish are commonly eaten. Tropical fruits and pastries are often enjoyed.

Fried coconut bread called *mandazi* is a popular breakfast. Lunch or dinner may include *ndizi nyama*, a stew made with fried plantains, meat or fish, and vegetables. *Mchuzi wa samaki* is a popular fish curry dish in Zanzibar. *Pilau*, or spicy cooked rice, is served at celebrations. *Mchicha* is a common side dish of dark leafy greens in rich sauce.

NDIZI NYAMA

MCHICHA

MANDAZI

Mandazi are similar to donuts! Have an adult help you make them.

Ingredients:

1 cup warm coconut milk
1/4 cup vegetable oil
1/4 cup white sugar
1 egg
2 teaspoons instant yeast

1/2 teaspoon salt
1/2 teaspoon ground cardamom
3 1/2 cups sifted flour
vegetable oil for frying

Steps:

1. Combine all ingredients, except the sifted flour, in a bowl.

2. Add the flour to the mixture one cup at a time. Mix until a dough forms. Knead the dough on a surface until it is no longer sticky.

3. Put the dough back in the bowl. Cover it with a dishcloth and let it rise in a warm place for about an hour.

4. Put the dough on a cutting surface and divide it to make four balls.

5. Take a ball and roll it out into a thin circle. Cut the flat dough circle into four triangles. Repeat with the remaining balls of dough.

6. Heat oil in a large saucepan. Fry three to four triangles at a time for about 1 to 2 minutes on each side. They should puff up and become golden brown.

7. Dry the fried mandazi with paper towels and serve warm.

Tanzanians celebrate many religious holidays. Christians honor Easter and Christmas by attending church. They enjoy large meals with family and friends. Muslims celebrate Ramadan in the spring. They **fast** for a month. A three-day feast called *Eid al-Fitr* marks the end of the fast.

Tanzanians also celebrate Union Day on April 26. Parades around the country mark the day Zanzibar and Tanganyika became one nation. The *Sauti za Busara* festival held in Zanzibar in February celebrates African music. Tanzania's different ethnic groups celebrate the harvest season, wildlife **migrations**, and the arts. Tanzanians are proud of their rich culture and traditions!

UNION DAY

SAUTI ZA BUSARA

1699
Omani Arabs remove the Portuguese from Zanzibar

AROUND 700 CE
Arab settlers arrive on the coast of present-day Tanzania

1919
Britain gains control of mainland Tanzania after Germany loses World War I

1886
Germany gains control over Tanganyika, now known as mainland Tanzania, and Britain begins control over Zanzibar

1506
The Portuguese gain control of most of the East African coast

1961
Mainland Tanzania becomes independent, with Zanzibar following two years later

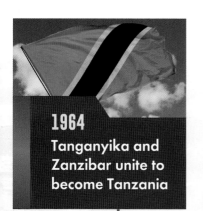

1964
Tanganyika and Zanzibar unite to become Tanzania

2010
Tanzania joins its neighbors in forming the East African Common Market to improve the region's economy

1995
Benjamin Mkapa is chosen president in Tanzania's first multi-party election

2021
Samia Suluhu Hassan becomes the first female president of Tanzania

TANZANIA FACTS

Official Name: United Republic of Tanzania

Flag of Tanzania: The Tanzanian flag is divided diagonally down the middle by a black band with yellow edges. A green triangle appears in the upper left corner. A light blue triangle appears in the lower right corner. Green represents Tanzania's plants, and blue stands for bodies of water. Black represents the Swahili people, and yellow is for the country's valuable resources.

Area: 365,755 square miles
  (947,300 square kilometers)

Capital City: Dodoma

Important Cities: Dar es Salaam, Zanzibar, Mwanza, Arusha

Population:
  63,852,892

WHERE PEOPLE LIVE

COUNTRYSIDE
63.3%

CITY
36.7%

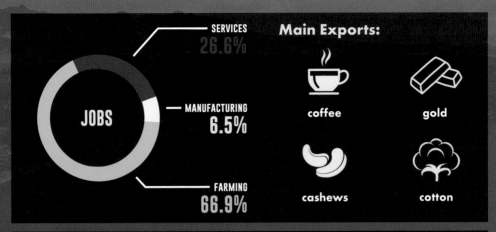

SERVICES
26.6%

JOBS

MANUFACTURING
6.5%

FARMING
66.9%

Main Exports:

coffee

gold

cashews

cotton

National Holiday:
Union Day, April 26

Main Languages:
Kiswahili and English

Form of Government:
presidential republic

Title for Country Leader:
president (chief of state and head of government)

RELIGION

MUSLIM
34.1%

OTHER
1.7%

FOLK
RELIGION
1.1%

CHRISTIAN
63.1%

Unit of Money:
Tanzanian shilling

GLOSSARY

ancestors—relatives who lived long ago

Arabs—people who are originally from the Arabian Peninsula and who now live mostly in the Middle East and Africa

archipelago—a group of islands

cuisine—a style of cooking

culture—the beliefs, arts, and ways of life in a place or society

ethnic—related to a group of people who share customs and an identity

fast—to stop eating all foods or particular foods for a time

humid—having a lot of moisture in the air

mainland—the main part of a country or continent

migrations—acts of traveling from one place to another, often with the seasons

plain—a large area of flat land

plantations—large farms that grow coffee beans, cotton, rubber, or other crops; plantations are mainly found in warm climates.

plateau—an area of flat, raised land

rural—related to the countryside

souvenirs—items that are reminders of places or events

staples—widely used foods or other items

tourism—the business of people traveling to visit other places

traditional—related to customs, ideas, or beliefs handed down from one generation to the next

tropical—part of the tropics; the tropics is a hot, rainy region near the equator.

urban—related to cities and city life

TO LEARN MORE

AT THE LIBRARY

Heale, Jay, Winnie Wong, and Kelly Spence. *Tanzania.* New York, N.Y.: Cavendish Square Publishing, 2018.

Hyde, Natalie. *Serengeti Research Journal.* New York, N.Y.: Crabtree Publishing Company, 2018.

Meinking, Mary. *Cheetahs.* Lake Elmo, Minn.: Focus Readers, 2018.

ON THE WEB

FACTSURFER

Factsurfer.com gives you a safe, fun way to find more information.

1. Go to www.factsurfer.com.

2. Enter "Tanzania" into the search box and click Q.

3. Select your book cover to see a list of related content.

INDEX

The images in this book are reproduced through the courtesy of: meunierd, front cover; MOIZ HUSEIN STORYTELLER, pp. 4-5; Steve Lagreca, p. 5 (Kilimanjaro National Park); H.-J. Petschke, p. 5 (Lake Manyara National Park); Olha Solodenko, p. 5 (The Old Fort); Christian Nieke, p. 5 (Selous Game Reserve); Andrzej Kubik, p. 8; Shujaa_777, p. 9 (Great Rift Valley); Blossfeldia, p. 9 (Dodoma); Eric Isselee, p. 10 (hippopotamus); Jearu, p. 10 (dik-dik); SanderMeertins, p. 10 (black-bellied starling); Maggy Meyer, p. 10 (African lion); nwdph, p. 11 (Masai giraffe); Anca Milushev, p. 12; Wikicommons, p. 13 (Saida Karoli); Elen Marlen, p. 13 (Zanzibar); derejeb, p. 14; intek1, p. 15; Jake Lyell/ Alamy, pp. 16, 20 (netball); ton koene/ Alamy, p. 17; Avatar_023, p. 18; imageBROKER/ Alamy, pp. 19 (tourism), 29 (shilling); Aleksandar Todorovic, p. 19 (Maasai herder); Katiekk, p. 20 (soccer); Charles O. Cecil/ Alamy, p. 21 (bao); SelimBT, p. 22 (making ugali); Freda Muyambo / Stockimo/ Alamy, p. 23 (ndizi nyama); Fanfo 687834658, p. 23 (mchicha); Sokor Space, p. 23 (mandazi); Ericky Boniphace/ Alamy, p. 24; YASUYOSHI CHIBA / Contributor/ Getty Images, pp. 24-25; Tatohra, p. 27 (1964); REUTERS/ Alamy, p. 27 (1995); Abaca Press/ Alamy, p. 27 (2021).